M

4/79

Merry Merry FIBruary

Merry Merry FIBruary

written by Doris Orgel

illustrations by Arnold Lobel

Parents' Magazine Press
New York

Library of Congress Cataloging in Publication Data
Orgel, Doris.
    Merry merry FIBruary.
    SUMMARY: The funniest things occur in the month of
FIBruary—fish go peopling, snow turns to ice-cream, and babies
are delivered by rocket.
    [1. Nonsense verses] I. Lobel, Arnold. II. Title.
PZ8.3.O68Me   811'.5'4 [811]   77-650
ISBN 0-8193-0900-1   ISBN 0-8193-0901-X lib. bdg.

Merry Merry FIBruary

n the month of FIBruary,
Fairest month in all the year,
Streets are paved with peanut brittle,
Rainbows bend from ear to ear.

Buttered bagels grow on bushes,
Elephants can dance the twist,
Ducks play bongos, cats can tango,
Rain's champagne—so's dew and mist.

On the first of FIBruary,
Setting out from Hackensack,
My Aunt Selma, in a seashell,
Sailed to Samarkand and back.

In FIBruary, Uncle Harry
Found no reason why he should
Spend his whole life as a grown-up—
And grew back down to babyhood.

On the third of FIBruary,
Lo! The leopard changed his spots
To pussy willows, tiger lilies,
Foxgloves and forget-me-nots.

All the FIBruary babies
From Biloxi to New York
Are delivered via rocket
By the busy Dr. Stork.

In FIBruary, Old MacDonald
Had an egg called Speckled Jen.
Ee-Ii-yO—it laid a little
Hen upon hen upon hen.

Here's a FIBruary finding:
Giants shrink and midgets grow.
Take Fee-Fi-Fo and Tiny Tom,
Though which is which I do not know.

In FIBruary, when it freezes,
Mount McKinley and Mount Snow
Are vanilla at the top,
And down below, pistachio.

THE FIRST WEEK

FIBRUARY

SUN	MON	TUE	WED	THU	FRI	SAT

Every FIBruary Zoo Day,
All the animals must wear
Shoes and socks and pants and dresses—
You and me, though, we go bare.

In FIBruary, my canary,
Who till then had never yet
Sung a single trill or burble,
Sang *Aida* at the Met.

For FIBruary Fill-Me-Up Day,
After dinner, as dessert,
I ate fifty jelly doughnuts—
Yet my belly did not hurt.

By mid-FIBruary moonlight,
My new neighbor, Billy Frink,
Grew petunias in his bathtub
And took showers in the sink.

On FIBruary Fair-and-Foul Day
Aunt Marie and Uncle Mike,
Who disagree on everything,
Both have weather that they like.

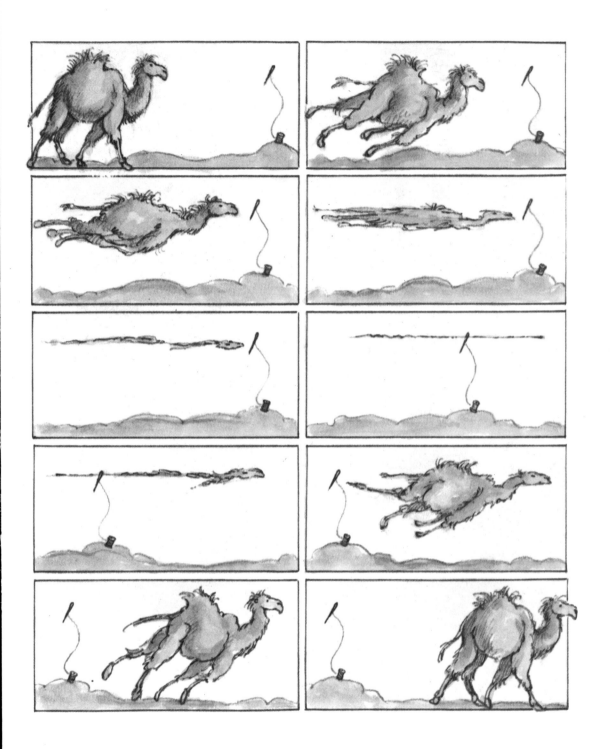

In dromedary FIBruary,
Though we heard a camel call,
"This needle's eye is far too narrow,"
He got through it—hump and all!

In Aquari-FIBruary,
Down Canal Street, wearing grins,
Swam my mama, and my grandma,
Showing off their four fine fins.

THE SECOND WEEK

FIBRUARY

SUN	MON	TUE	WED	THU	FRI	SAT

Any FIBruary morning,
See my nimble Grandpa Phil,
Ninety-three, still turning cartwheels
On his narrow windowsill.

On a FIBruary Monday,
Great-Aunt Bess became a bus:
Grew tires, fenders, windshield wipers,
And gave rides to all of us.

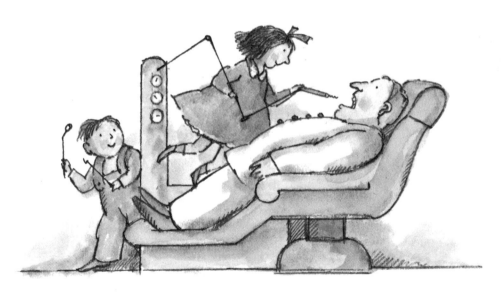

On a FIBruary Toothday,
Dentist, open wider, please.
Now sit still and do not wiggle
While I fill *your* cavities.

In FIBruary, any Wind's Day,
Any wind, from coast to coast,
May just come along and blow you
Where you want to go the most.

On a FIBruary Thirstday,
After eating pizza pie,
Though I drank up Lake Superior,
My interior still felt dry.

At the gym in FIBruary,
My athletic sister, Rose,
Wears her sneakers on her fingers
And shoots baskets with her toes.

On Tattersday, come wearing any
Torn and raggedy old thing.
Just bring a crown along, and be
A FIBruary Fashion King.

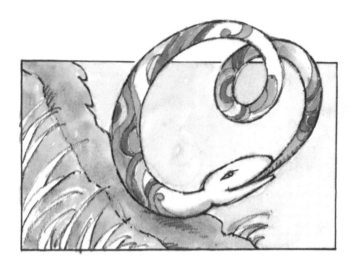

On FIBruary's Loop-de-Loop Day,
Tail tucked tight into its mouth,
Rolls a reptile called the hoop snake
Down a mountain, heading South.

For the FIBruary dog show,
My retriever, good old Fred—
Also partly dachshund, spitz
and chow—becomes a thoroughbred.

A noble prince, but very homely,
Whose reflection scared him numb,
Kissed it and—behold!—became
Fairest frog in FIBrudom.

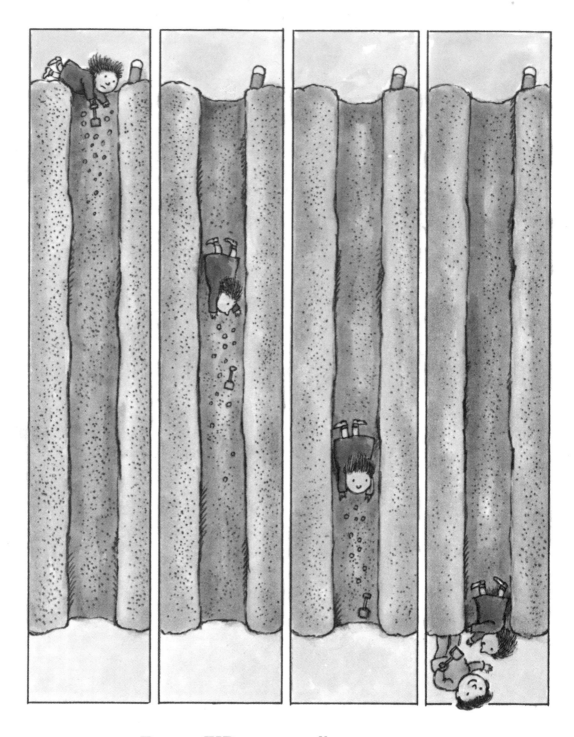

From a FIBruary sandbox
Disappeared my Cousin Dinah:
Dug a little hole—*kerplunk!*
Tumbled in, and fell to China.

In a FIBruary blizzard
Sighed a sad-eyed centipede,
"Only ninety-nine galoshes—
That's one fewer than I need!"

If you swim in FIBruary
Near San Pablo Bay, beware:
Don't bite on any bait or hook,
Because fish go peopling there.

On the last—the twenty-eighth day—
My old pencil had a fit
And wrote all these silly verses—
Don't blame me for them: Blame it.
And if ever you feel fibful,
From my pencil take a cue:
Add a day to FIBruary
With a fancy fib or two.

THE FOURTH WEEK

FIBRUARY

SUN	MON	TUE	WED	THU	FRI	SAT

An astute reviewer and former editor of children's books, DORIS ORGEL is the author of many distinguished picture books and stories for older readers, including an ALA Notable Book, *A Certain Magic*, in 1976. Mrs. Orgel is also a gifted translator of tales—among them Walter Grieder's *The Enchanted Drum* for Parents' Magazine Press. *Merry Merry FIBruary* is her first original work for Parents'. The author lives in Westport, Connecticut.

ARNOLD LOBEL has been writing and illustrating books for children ever since he graduated from Pratt Institute in Brooklyn, New York. Ranked among this country's most gifted picture-book artists, he illustrated *Junk Day on Juniper Street*, *The Magic Spectacles* and three *Miss Suzy* books for Parents' Magazine Press. He is also the author/illustrator of *The Ice-Cream Cone Coot and Other Rare Birds*.